# BEADING

## Bracelets, Earrings, Necklaces and More

Written by Judy Ann Sadler

Illustrated by Tracy Walker

KIDS CAN PRESS LTD.

TORONTO

To Mom and Dad Sadler, for threading our lives
with beads of wisdom, goodness and love

**Canadian Cataloguing in Publication Data**

Sadler, Judy Ann, 1959–
Beading : bracelets, earrings, necklaces and more

(Kids can crafts)
ISBN 1-55074-338-4 (pbk.)

1. Beadwork — Juvenile literature.   2. Jewelry making
— Juvenile literature.   I. Walker, Tracy.   II. Title.

TT860.S33  1996     j745.594'2     C96-930724-1

Kids Can Press Ltd.
29 Birch Avenue
Toronto, Ontario, Canada
M4V 1E2

Edited by Laurie Wark
Designed by Karen Powers
Photography by Frank Baldasarra
Printed in Hong Kong

96 0 9 8 7 6 5 4 3 2

# Contents

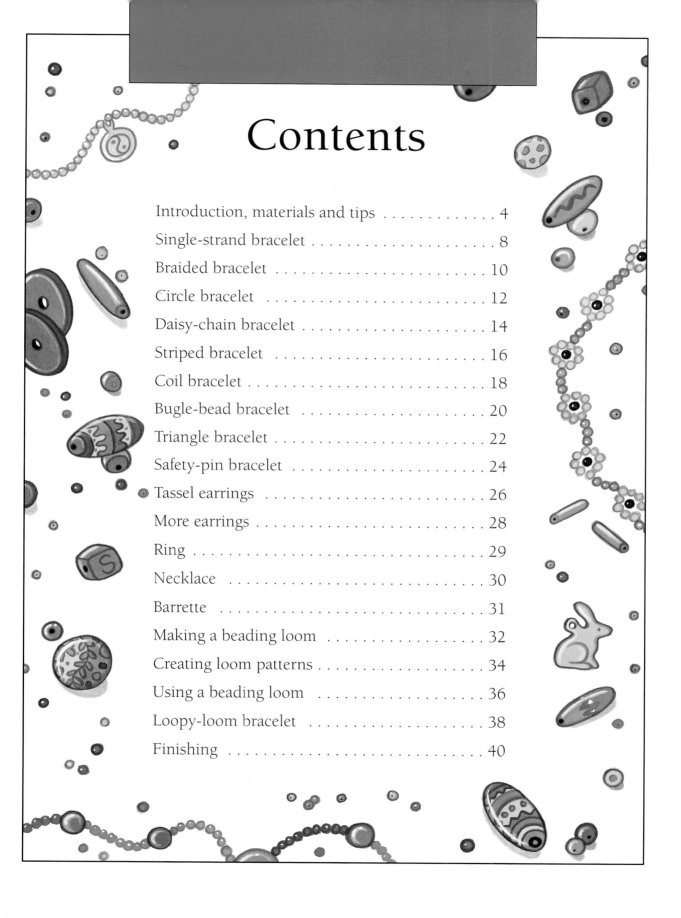

Introduction, materials and tips . . . . . . . . . . . . 4

Single-strand bracelet . . . . . . . . . . . . . . . . . 8

Braided bracelet . . . . . . . . . . . . . . . . . . . . 10

Circle bracelet . . . . . . . . . . . . . . . . . . . . . 12

Daisy-chain bracelet . . . . . . . . . . . . . . . . . . 14

Striped bracelet . . . . . . . . . . . . . . . . . . . . 16

Coil bracelet . . . . . . . . . . . . . . . . . . . . . . 18

Bugle-bead bracelet . . . . . . . . . . . . . . . . . . 20

Triangle bracelet . . . . . . . . . . . . . . . . . . . . 22

Safety-pin bracelet . . . . . . . . . . . . . . . . . . . 24

Tassel earrings . . . . . . . . . . . . . . . . . . . . . 26

More earrings . . . . . . . . . . . . . . . . . . . . . 28

Ring . . . . . . . . . . . . . . . . . . . . . . . . . . . 29

Necklace . . . . . . . . . . . . . . . . . . . . . . . . 30

Barrette . . . . . . . . . . . . . . . . . . . . . . . . . 31

Making a beading loom . . . . . . . . . . . . . . . . 32

Creating loom patterns . . . . . . . . . . . . . . . . 34

Using a beading loom . . . . . . . . . . . . . . . . . 36

Loopy-loom bracelet . . . . . . . . . . . . . . . . . . 38

Finishing . . . . . . . . . . . . . . . . . . . . . . . . 40

# Introduction

*Pick up some beads and roll them around in your hand. Beads on their own are lovely, but it's difficult to handle them without thinking of all their possibilities. This book is filled with ideas for how to thread, hang and weave beads to make wonderful jewellery. Create dangling earrings, unique necklaces or a wrist full of bracelets. All these items make great gifts, too. But beware — once you start beading it's hard to stop, so make sure you keep lots of supplies on hand. Explore your local craft or specialty bead store for interesting beads and findings. Be as creative as you like. The instructions will teach you some basic techniques and give you lots of suggestions, but there's always room for your own ideas.*
*Happy beading!*

## MATERIALS

SEED BEADS
You will need tiny seed beads for most of the projects in this book. They are inexpensive and come in a wide selection of colours and finishes, such as pearlized, metallic, silver-lined, clear and striped.

BUGLE BEADS
These are like long, thin seed beads. They come in many colours and finishes, as well as different lengths.

E BEADS
These beads are also known as small pony beads. They are larger than seed beads, but similar in shape and colour.

## OTHER BEADS

Collect unusual beads, charms, pendants and letters that can be used as special accents on your jewellery.

## THREAD

The best thread is strong, thin nylon beading thread. Some threads are too thick to thread twice through a seed bead, and that makes them unsuitable for patterns and beading looms. Clear beading thread and 1.82 or 2.25 kg (4 or 5 lb.) test fishing line are good for many projects, especially if you are using clear beads. You will need thin elastic cord for other projects.

## WIRE

You will need thin wire (28 to 34 gauge) and heavy wire (18 or 20 gauge) for some projects. You can find wire at hardware and craft stores.

## NEEDLES

Beading needles are long, thin and flexible. They make it easy to pick up beads for threading. Store needles in their original package or in a pin cushion.

## LOOM

Instructions are given in this book for turning a shoebox into a sturdy beading loom. You can also buy a standard loom at craft and hobby stores.

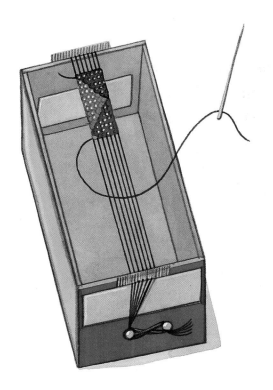

## CLASPS

There are many different types of clasps available for bracelets and necklaces. One of the best clasps for making bracelets is the spring ring used with a small tag. For necklaces, barrel clasps are good, too. Before you use a clasp, test it to make sure it works.

## EARRINGS

Head pins, eye pins, kidney wires, hooks, hoops and posts can be used in making earrings.

## PLIERS

You'll need a pair of needlenose pliers with side cutters when working with wire and for closing small metal clasp rings.

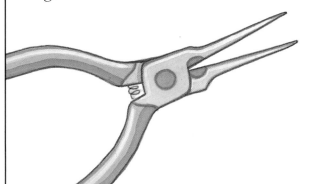

## TIPS

### TYING ON A CLASP

Use a double or triple knot to tie on each end of the clasp. When you begin a project, fasten the clasp before you tie it onto your work so that you'll have both parts on hand when you're finished.

### MAKING BRACELETS WITHOUT CLASPS

You can also make a bracelet without a clasp. Make it big enough to slip over your hand, or if you want to wear it all the time, simply tie it around your wrist. In either case, knot the thread ends together, draw them back through the last several beads, and trim them.

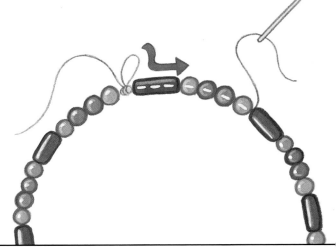

## SECURING KNOTS

Dab clear nail polish onto the knots you have tied to prevent them from coming undone. You can also use a strong, clear-drying waterproof glue, but be sure to follow the manufacturer's instructions.

## ANCHORING A BEAD

To prevent beads from falling off, loop your thread once or twice through a seed bead near the end of the thread. This anchor bead can be removed when you are finished beading if it doesn't match your pattern.

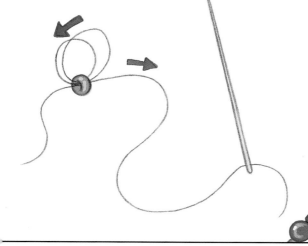

## SORTING AND STORING BEADS

Beads come in small bags or plastic vials and cases. Pour out a few at a time as you bead. Return beads to their containers when you are finished. Store all your bead packages in a box or in plastic containers. A fishing tackle box is a handy container because it has many small compartments. The beads won't get mixed up, and you can sort them according to colour and size. Use a small spoon to take beads from the compartments to your work surface, or use them directly from the box. You may find it easiest to thread on beads from a saucer or the palm of your hand.

## MAKING NECKLACES, CHOKERS AND ANKLETS

Most of the bracelet patterns in this book can be used to make necklaces, chokers and anklets, too. Use clasps on chokers or anklets and simply tie the ends together on a necklace.

# Single-strand bracelet

*Make this simple bracelet using only seed beads, or experiment by combining different types of beads in many sizes and colours.*

## YOU WILL NEED

- 40 cm (16 in.) of beading thread or fishing line
- a clasp (optional)
- beads
- a beading needle (optional)
- scissors
- clear nail polish

1 Use a triple knot to tie on a clasp about 10 cm (4 in.) from the end of the thread. Do not trim the thread. Anchor a bead onto the end if you are not using a clasp.

2 Decide on a pattern and start threading on beads, with or without a needle.

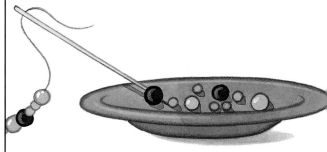

3 Measure the bracelet around your wrist and continue the pattern until the bracelet fits. Try to end the pattern so that it matches the beginning.

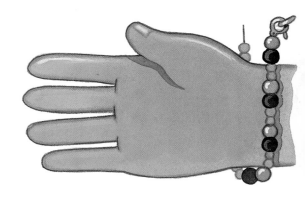

**4** If you are using a clasp, tie a ring or tag onto the other end, making the knot as close to the ring as you can. If you're not using a clasp, knot the ends together.

**5** Draw the thread end back through the last several beads on the bracelet. Trim the thread. Do the same for the other end.

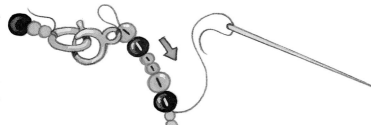

**6** Secure the knots with nail polish.

## OTHER IDEAS

🔴 Thread beads larger than seed beads onto elastic cord for a bracelet that slips easily over your hand and fits snugly on your wrist.

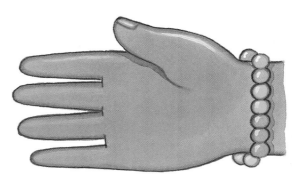

🔴 Make a necklace, choker or anklet.

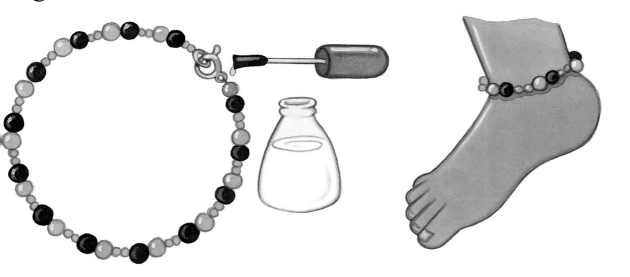

# Braided bracelet

*Try this bracelet with any three colours
you like. Gold, copper and silver
or red, black and yellow are
nice combinations.*

## YOU WILL NEED

- 2 pieces of beading thread or fishing line,
  each 80 cm (32 in.) long
- a clasp
- seed beads in three colours
- a beading needle (optional)
- scissors
- tape
- clear nail polish

1 Hold one end of each thread together and pull them through the clasp. Centre the clasp on the threads and fasten them securely with a triple knot.

2 Bead one of the threads until the beads overlap around your wrist by about 4 cm (1½ in.).

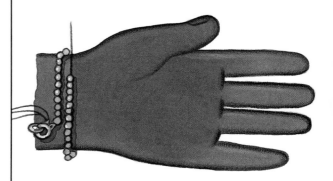

3 Draw the thread through the last bead one or two times to anchor it.

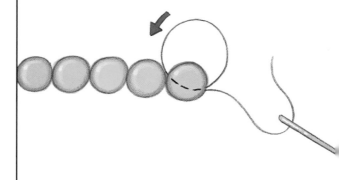

4 Bead two of the other threads to the same length as the first one. Anchor the last bead on each one.

5 Draw the fourth thread through several beads at the top of one of the beaded threads and trim it off.

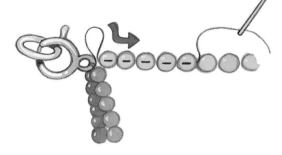

6 Tape the clasp to your work table (or ask someone to hold it). Make sure the beads on each thread are pushed up so that no thread shows between the beads.

7 Gently braid the beaded threads together. Hold the bracelet straight so that it does not twist or flip over.

8 When you reach the end, hold the threads together and try the bracelet around your wrist. It should be a little loose. Remove some beads if you need to make the bracelet smaller, or if you need to even up the strands.

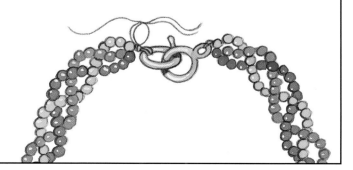

9 Hold two thread ends in one hand and one thread in the other. Tightly knot them together against the beads. Tie on the other end of the clasp and draw the ends back through the beads. Trim the ends. Secure the knots with nail polish.

# Circle bracelet

*Fishing line without a needle works well for this bracelet. If you don't have any, use beading thread with a needle on each end.*

## YOU WILL NEED

- 1 m (3 ft.) of fishing line
- a clasp (optional)
- seed beads in two colours
- scissors
- clear nail polish

**1** If you are using a clasp, thread and knot it onto the centre of your fishing line.

**2** Thread three beads of the same colour onto each end of the line. Thread one more bead of the same colour onto one of the lines. Poke through it from the opposite direction with the other line. Pull the lines in opposite directions so that the seven beads form a circle. Centre the circle on your line.

**3** Put one bead of the other colour onto one line. Poke through it from the opposite direction with the other line. Pull the lines in opposite directions until this bead meets the first ones.

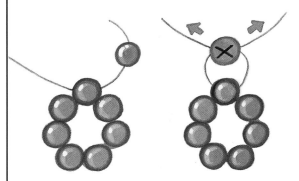

4 Thread three same-coloured beads onto each line. Thread one more on one line and poke through it from the opposite direction with the other line. Pull the lines in opposite directions to form a circle made of eight beads.

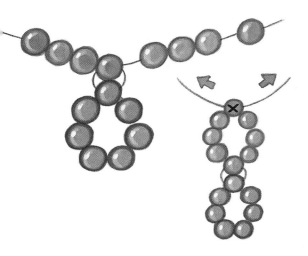

5 Change colours and continue making eight-bead circles until your bracelet fits.

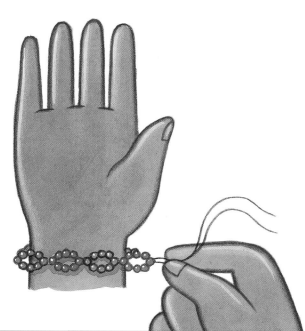

6 Fasten on the other end of the clasp. If you are not using a clasp, simply tie the end into the first circle. Poke the ends back through the closest beads and trim them. Secure the knots with nail polish.

## OTHER IDEAS

● Make this bracelet in one colour or in more than two colours.

● Make bracelets out of circles made from four or six beads, or try circles larger than eight beads.

# Daisy-chain bracelet

*These instructions use green, yellow and black seed beads. You can use any three colours, just change the colours named in the instructions to suit you.*

## YOU WILL NEED

- 1 m (3 ft.) of beading thread or fishing line
- a clasp (optional)
- green, yellow and black seed beads
- a beading needle
- scissors
- clear nail polish

1 If you are using a clasp, tie it 10 cm (4 in.) from the end of the thread. If you are not using a clasp, anchor a green bead 10 cm (4 in.) from the end.

2 Thread on three green beads (only two if you're not using a clasp) and eight yellow ones.

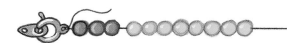

3 Bring the thread through the first yellow bead you put on. Go through it from the same direction, that is, from the side closest to the green beads. Pull the thread all the way through to make a circle and gently slide the circle as close to the green beads as possible.

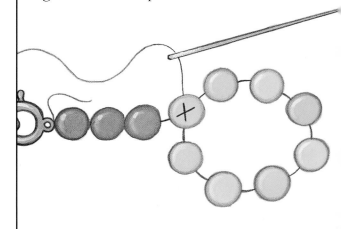

4 Thread on one black bead. Bring the thread through the yellow bead directly across from the first yellow one you threaded on, again from the same direction.

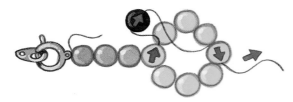

5 Pull on the thread and adjust the daisy so that the black bead is in the centre.

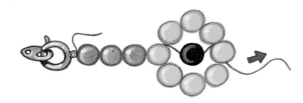

6 Thread on three more green beads and eight more yellow beads. Repeat from step 3 until the bracelet fits. Tie both ends together or tie on the other end of the clasp. Draw the ends through the last several beads, trim them and secure the knots with nail polish.

## OTHER IDEAS

● Make this bracelet with many different-coloured daisies. Or try the traditional green leaves and white flowers with yellow centres.

● Instead of putting three green beads between each daisy, put four or more. Or leave them out altogether for non-stop daisies.

● Use an E bead instead of a seed bead for the centre of the daisy. Or make the bracelet completely with E beads. Use six beads instead of eight to form each flower.

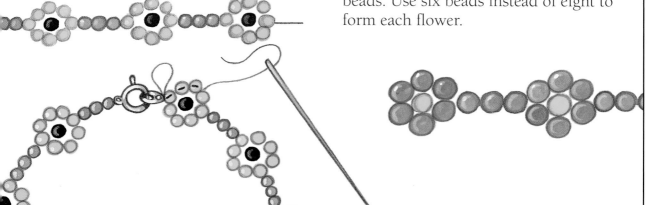

# Striped bracelet

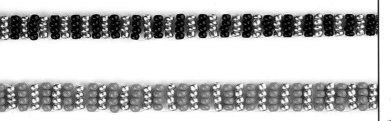

*Here's a patterned bracelet that you don't need a loom to make. It's best to use beading thread for this bracelet since fishing line can be too stiff.*

## YOU WILL NEED

- 1 m (3 ft.) of beading thread
- 2 beading needles
- seed beads in two colours
- a clasp
- scissors
- clear nail polish

1 Thread each end of the beading thread through a needle.

2 At one end of the thread, put on two beads of the same colour, the clasp and two more beads of the same colour.

3 Thread on four more beads in the other colour, but before they slide all the way down, pass through them with the other needle in the opposite direction.

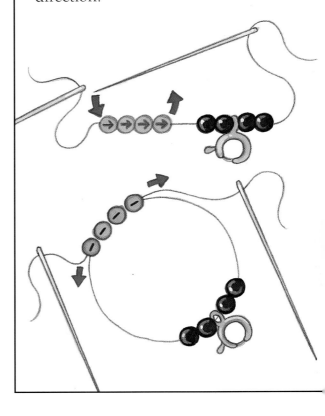

**4** Centre the two rows of beads on the thread.

**5** Continue the striped pattern, threading the beads on one of the needles and passing through them in the opposite direction with the other needle.

**6** When the bracelet is the right length, tie on the other end of the clasp. Trim the ends and secure the knots with nail polish.

## OTHER DESIGNS

● Knot a clasp in the centre of 1 m (3 ft.) of beading thread or fishing line. Hold the ends together and thread on a seed bead. Separate the threads and string three seed beads of a different colour onto each thread. Hold the threads together again and string on another seed bead. Continue in this way until the bracelet fits. Fasten on the other end of the clasp, draw the ends back through the last several beads, trim them and secure the knots with nail polish.

● Try this one without a clasp. Thread two seed beads onto one end of 1 m (3 ft.) of beading thread or fishing line and centre them. Hold the ends together and thread on three beads of a different colour. Separate the lines and thread one seed bead onto each line. Bring the lines together again and thread on three more seed beads. Continue in this way until the bracelet fits. Tie the bracelet together, draw the ends back through the last several beads, trim them and secure the knot with nail polish.

# Coil bracelet

*This bracelet is quick to make and easily adjusts to fit any size of wrist.*

## YOU WILL NEED

- 40 cm (16 in.) of 18 or 20 gauge heavy wire
- needlenose pliers
- E beads (or other similarly sized beads with large holes)
- an empty bathroom tissue roll

1 Use the pliers to bend a loop at one end of the wire.

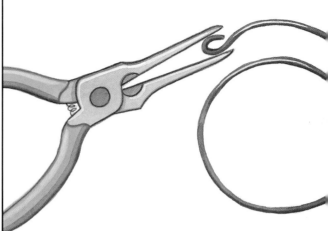

2 Put on a bead with a hole large enough to cover the bent-over end. The loop should be large enough to hold the bead in place.

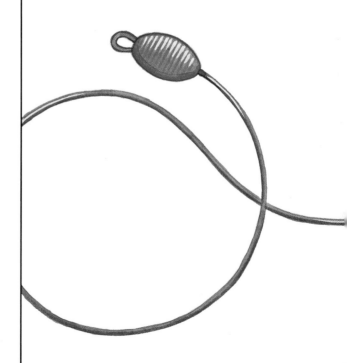

3 Holding beads in your hand, thread them onto the wire until you almost reach the end.

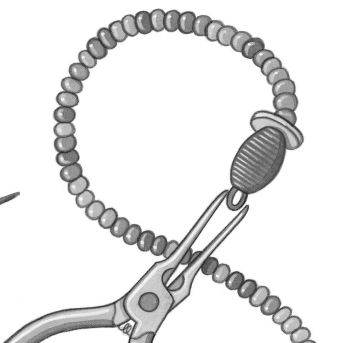

4 Put on a bead with a hole large enough to cover the end of the wire as you bend it into a loop. There should be some movement between the beads.

5 Coil the beaded wire around the bathroom tissue roll. Remove it and adjust your coil bracelet to fit over your hand onto your wrist.

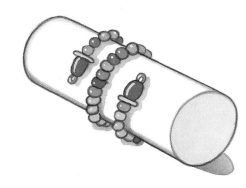

## OTHER IDEAS

● Make a beaded bangle. Cut about 23 cm (9 in.) of wire and follow steps 1 to 3. Bend the beaded wire into a circle and slide it over your hand onto your wrist to see if it fits. To close the bangle, bring the end through the loop and bend it into a loop, too. Use the pliers to trim the wire if necessary. Tuck the end into the last bead.

# Bugle-bead bracelet

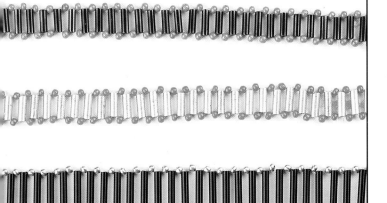

*Bugle beads look great with seed beads. It's best to use fishing line for this bracelet because thread will show.*

## YOU WILL NEED

- 1.5 m (5 ft.) of fishing line
- a clasp
- seed beads
- bugle beads 0.5 to 1 cm (¼ to ½ in.) long
- scissors
- clear nail polish

1 Centre the clasp on the line. Poke the line through the clasp again and tie it in a triple knot.

2 Hold the ends together and thread on two seed beads.

3 Separate the lines and thread a bugle bead onto one of them. Poke the other line into the other end of the bugle bead. Pull the ends in opposite directions.

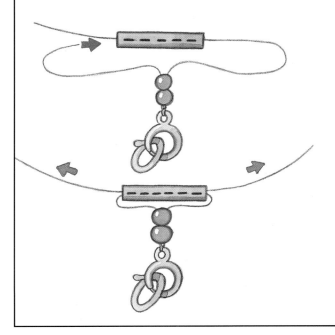

**4** String a seed bead onto each line.

**5** Thread on another bugle bead and continue until the bracelet fits your wrist.

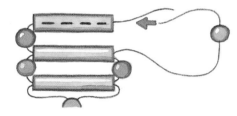

**6** Finish by holding the two ends together and threading on two seed beads. Tie on the other end of the clasp in a triple knot. Trim the threads and secure the knots with nail polish.

## OTHER IDEAS

● Bugle beads come in many different lengths. Try shorter or longer ones to make this bracelet.

● Tie and glue a strip of this bugle-bead design onto a hair barrette.

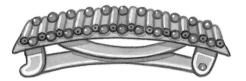

● Instead of starting this bracelet with two seed beads threaded together, separate the lines and thread five seed beads on each line. Bring the lines together and thread on one more seed bead, a bugle bead and another seed bead. Separate them again and thread five more seed beads on each line. Continue this pattern until the bracelet fits your wrist.

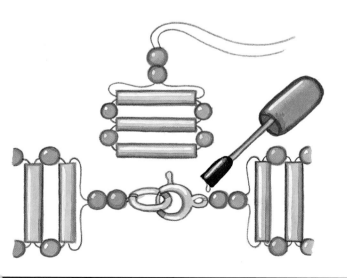

# Triangle bracelet

*Once you've formed a couple of triangles, you'll be surprised at how quickly you can make this unique bracelet.*

## YOU WILL NEED

- 1.5 m (5 ft.) of beading thread or fishing line
- a clasp (optional)
- a beading needle
- bugle beads
- seed beads
- scissors
- clear nail polish

1 Tie the clasp on one end of the thread, leaving a 10-cm (4-in.) tail to be woven in later. If you are not using a clasp, anchor a seed bead 10 cm (4 in.) from one end.

2 Alternate threading on a bugle bead then a seed bead until you have three of each.

3 Loop the thread around and go back through the first bugle bead and then the first seed bead. Enter the beads from the clasp side. This will form a triangle.

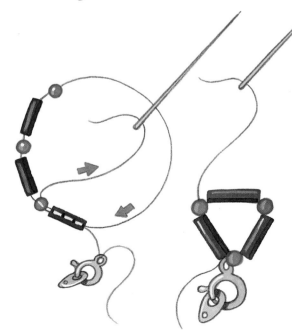

4 Thread on another bugle bead, seed bead and bugle bead. Bring the thread through a seed bead, as shown.

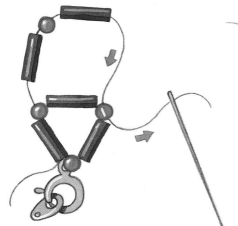

5 Thread on another bugle bead, seed bead and bugle bead. Again, bring the thread through the seed bead. Arrange the beads in triangles, so that one triangle has the pointed end up and the next has the pointed end down.

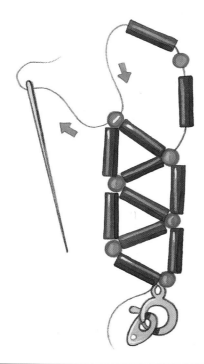

6 Continue until the bracelet fits your wrist. Draw the thread back through the last bugle bead you put on.

7 Tie on the other end of the clasp or remove the anchor bead and knot the threads together. Weave in the threads and trim them. Secure the knots with nail polish.

## OTHER IDEAS

🌑 Use different-coloured bugle beads so that the beads along the top and bottom are different from the beads in the middle.

# Safety-pin bracelet

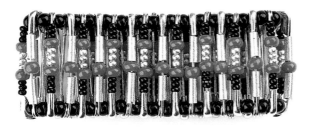

*This shiny, comfortable bracelet is fun to put together and it looks terrific. Make one bracelet with silver safety pins and another with gold pins.*

## YOU WILL NEED

- about 35 safety pins
- bugle beads
- seed beads
- tape
- 2 pieces of gold, silver or white thin elastic cord each 30 cm (12 in.) long
- E beads or beads of a similar size
- measuring tape
- scissors
- clear nail polish

1 Carefully open each safety pin and thread on bugle beads and seed beads in any pattern you like. Close the pins as you go.

2 Tape the end of one piece of elastic cord to your work table.

3 Poke the free end of the elastic through the round hole at the bottom of a beaded safety pin. Thread on an E bead, too.

4 Thread on another pin, but this time go through the hole at the top of the pin. Thread on another E bead.

5 Repeat steps 3 and 4. Make sure the beads on the pins are all facing outwards.

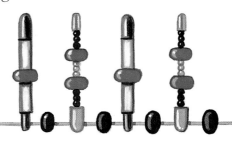

**6** Measure your wrist and add 2 cm (¾ in.). This is how long your bracelet should be. As you reach this length, end with a pin threaded through the top and an E bead.

**7** Remove the tape from the elastic cord and knot the ends together.

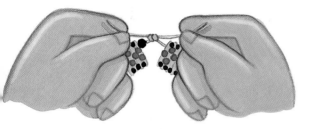

**8** Thread the other piece of elastic through all the free ends of the pins, putting an E bead between each pin and one at the end. Tie the ends together.

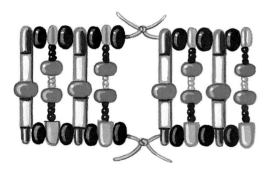

**9** Trim the ends and secure the knots with nail polish.

## OTHER IDEAS

● Hang a couple of beaded safety pins on a pair of earring hooks or from a necklace.

● Use two beads between each safety pin.

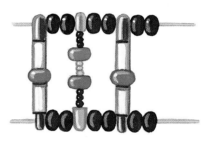

● Try larger safety pins with larger beads.

# Tassel earrings

*After you've made these basic earrings, try making tassels with beads in different colours and sizes or make the tassels longer.*

## YOU WILL NEED

- beading thread
- scissors
- a beading needle
- seed beads
- 2 head pins
- 2 earring caps
- 2 earring wires
- white liquid glue
- needlenose pliers

1 Cut 16 pieces of beading thread, each 30 cm (12 in.) long. Thread one of them into the needle.

2 Hold the end of the thread in one hand as you pick up 20 beads with the needle in your other hand.

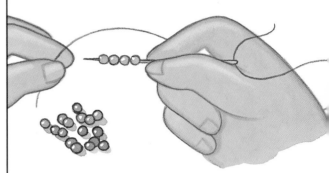

3 Bring the needle back through all the beads except for the last three you put on.

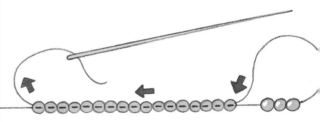

4 Make the ends even by holding them together and pulling gently on the beads. There should be a flower-shaped trio of beads at the end of the thread.

**5** Make 15 more beaded threads.

**6** Divide the beaded threads into two groups of eight. Hold them by the threads and adjust them so that they hang evenly.

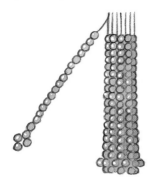

**7** Use an overhand knot to tie the threads together as close to the beads as you can. Before you tighten the knot, poke a head pin into it.

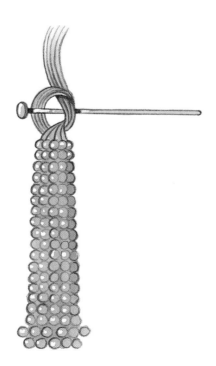

**8** Trim the threads close to the knot. Put a drop of glue onto the knot.

**9** Poke the head pin into the hole in the earring cap. Use pliers to cut the pin so that it is about 1.5 cm (⅝ in.) long.

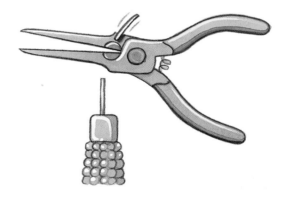

**10** Bend the pin into a loop. Hang the tassel on an earring wire. Finish the other earring.

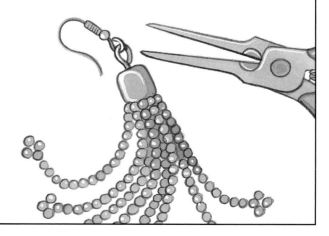

# More earrings

*Explore your local craft or specialty bead store for interesting beads, and try these ideas.*

### BEADED PIN

Bead a head or eye pin, bend the end into a loop and hang it on an earring wire. Since these are so simple to make, bead many pins to match your clothes and mood. Hang different pins on your earrings each day!

### HOOPS

There are commercial hoops available that are easy to bead into earrings. Open one by pulling one side of the wire circle out of the connecting piece. (The other side is fastened closed and does not open.) Choose a variety of beads to hang on the hoop. Mix and match shapes, sizes and colours. Close the hoop and use pliers to pinch the connecting piece closed so that the wire cannot pop open. Hang the hoop on an earring wire.

# Ring

2 Thread four more beads on one end, but before they slide down the wire, draw the other end through them from the opposite direction. Pull the wires so that the beads rest above the four beads already on the wire.

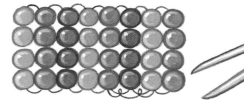

3 Continue until the ring is the right size. Thread one end through the first four beads to create a circle. Weave the ends up the side. Use pliers to trim the ends and bend them so that there are no sharp points.

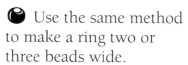

## YOU WILL NEED

- 70 cm (28 in.) of
28 to 34 gauge thin wire
- seed beads
- needlenose pliers

1 Thread four beads onto the wire and centre them.

## OTHER IDEAS

🔘 Use the same method to make a ring two or three beads wide.

🔘 Bead enough of a 25-cm (10-in.) piece of thread to make a ring. Knot it tightly, weave in the ends and trim them. Make sure it isn't too tight on your finger.

# Necklace

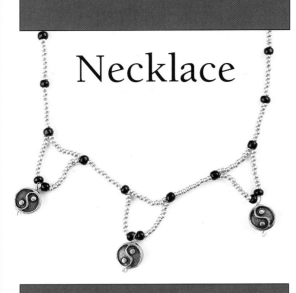

2 Separate the threads and put ten seed beads on each one. On one thread add an E bead, charm, E bead and ten more seed beads. If a charm hangs sideways on the necklace, remove it and use pliers to add on a jump ring.

3 Hold the thread ends together again and thread on an E bead, ten seed beads and another E bead. Separate the threads again and continue steps 2 and 3 until you have three charms on the necklace.

## YOU WILL NEED

- 2 pieces of beading thread or fishing line each 1 m (3 ft.) long
- seed beads • E beads
- 3 charms or pendants
- a beading needle (optional) • a clasp
- scissors • clear nail polish

1 Hold the thread ends together and anchor a seed bead 20 cm (8 in.) from the end. On the other end, thread ten seed beads and an E bead. Continue this pattern until you have five sections ending with an E bead.

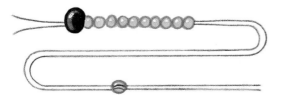

4 Thread on five more sections of seed beads and E beads. Remove the anchor bead. Try the necklace around your neck, and add enough beads onto each end until it fits.

5 Before you add the clasp, pull on each end until there is no thread showing between the beads. Tie a part of the clasp onto each end. Draw the ends into the last several beads, trim them and secure the knots with nail polish.

# Barrette

### YOU WILL NEED

- 3 m (10 ft.) of fishing line
- a beading needle
- a plain barrette
- beads in various colours and sizes
- scissors • clear nail polish

1 Hold the ends of the fishing line together and thread them into the needle. Poke the looped end of the line through the hole in one end of the barrette. Draw the needle through this loop and pull it until the fishing line is fastened to the side of the barrette.

2 Thread a couple of beads (or one large bead) onto your line. Thread the line through the barrette and position the bead where you want it.

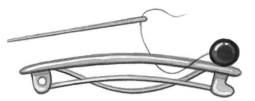

3 Keep threading on beads and winding the line around and through the barrette. You may need to go back and forth across the barrette a few times to fill all the spaces.

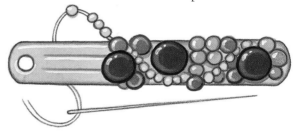

4 Finish beading at one end of the barrette and bring the line through the hole. Separate the lines and thread just one line through the hole again. Knot the ends together, weave them through some of the criss-crossed lines on the underside of the barrette and trim them. Secure the knot with nail polish.

# Making a beading loom

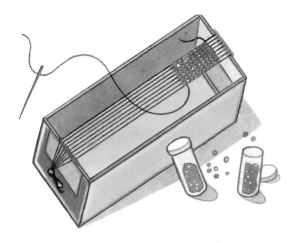

*A beading loom allows you to create all kinds of intricate beaded patterns. Once you've made this simple beading loom, turn the page to find out how to use it.*

## YOU WILL NEED

- a shoebox at least 20 cm (8 in.) long
- scissors • a ruler • glue
- corrugated cardboard
- 3 paper fasteners 2.5 cm (1 in.) or longer
- strong tape, such as cloth, duct or electrical tape
- about 30 round toothpicks

1 Carefully use open scissors to poke a small hole in the middle of one end of the shoebox, about 2.5 cm (1 in.) up from the bottom.

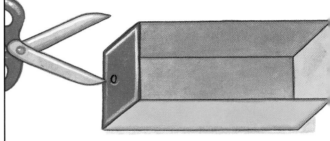

2 In the other end, poke two small holes about 3 cm (1¼ in.) apart, about 2.5 cm (1 in.) up from the bottom.

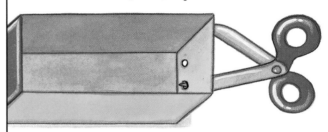

3 Measure, cut and glue in pieces of corrugated cardboard to reinforce the inside of the box. Glue in the end pieces first, followed by the sides and then the bottom.

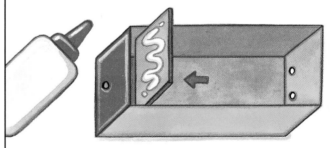

4 Use the scissors to poke through the end holes you made, but this time go through the corrugated cardboard too.

**5** Poke a paper fastener into each hole and open it on the inside. Cover the open fastener ends with tape.

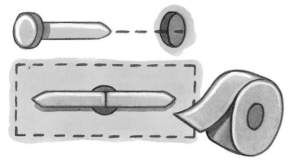

**6** Break or cut the round toothpicks in half. Hold each half toothpick over a garbage can as you trim off the very end to get rid of the sharp tip.

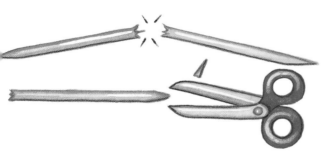

**7** Place a piece of tape, sticky side up, on your work surface. Line 30 of the half toothpicks side by side on the tape with the tips even and about 0.5 cm (¼ in.) over the edge of the tape.

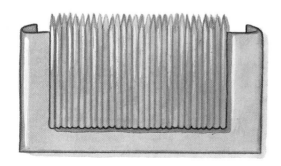

**8** Spread glue along the toothpicks. Lift the toothpick tape and centre it along one end of the shoebox so that the toothpicks are about 0.5 cm (¼ in.) above the edge of the box. Do the same for the other end of the box with the remaining 30 half toothpicks. Add extra tape if you need it. Let the glue dry.

## OTHER IDEAS

● If you have two small pocket combs, you can glue and tape one on each end of the shoebox instead of using toothpicks.

● If you have a small wooden crate (such as the type tangerines are packed in), use it instead of a shoebox. Hammer small nails into the ends in place of paper fasteners. Instead of using toothpicks, score evenly spaced notches in the ends with open scissors.

# Creating loom patterns

*Stripes, diagonals, checkers, flowers, zigzags, diamonds, initials, numbers and figures are only a few of the designs possible on a loom.*

## MAKING A PATTERN

Use graph paper (or lined paper to which you have added vertical and more horizontal lines) and pencil crayons or markers to map out your own design. Each square on the graph paper represents a bead on the loom. Experiment until you are happy with your pattern.

## FOLLOWING A PATTERN

It's easiest to follow your pattern by turning it to the vertical position beside your loom. Start in the top left corner. If your pattern starts with a blue bead followed by three red beads and a yellow one, that is the order you should thread beads onto your needle. Follow the pattern row by row until you are finished or your work is the length you want it to be.

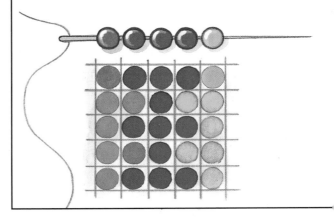

# LOOM PATTERNS

Here are some sample patterns you can follow. When you've decided what your bracelet will look like, turn the page to find out how to set up the loom.

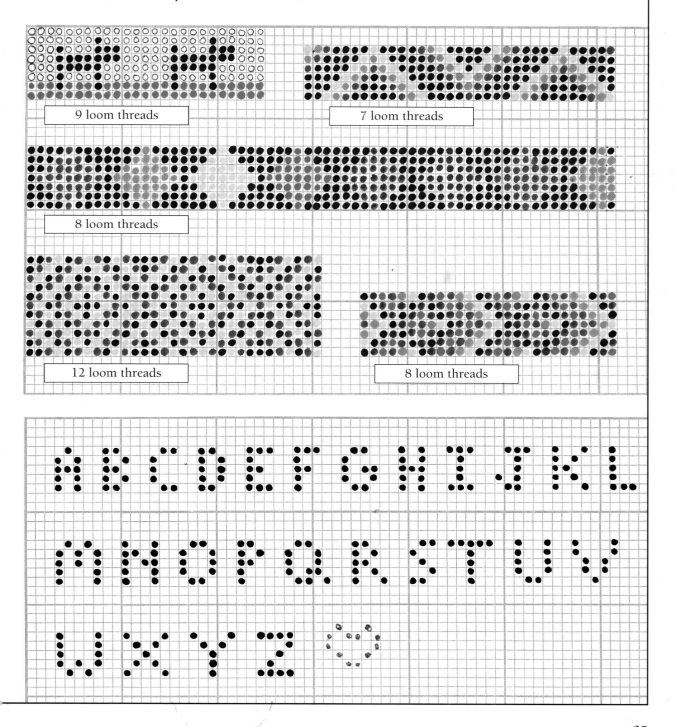

9 loom threads

7 loom threads

8 loom threads

12 loom threads

8 loom threads

# Using a beading loom

*You'll be surprised at how simple it is to learn the centuries-old traditional art of bead weaving using a loom. Use beading thread rather than fishing line on your loom.*

## YOU WILL NEED

- a shoebox loom (or store-bought)
- beading thread
- scissors
- a ruler or measuring tape
- a rubber band
- a beading needle
- seed beads

1  Cut your beading threads 30 cm (12 in.) longer than the length of your loom. You will need one more thread than you have rows of beads in your pattern. So if your pattern is six beads wide, you'll need seven threads.

2  Hold all the ends of your threads together and make an overhand knot. Hook this knot around the single paper fastener at one end of the loom.

3  Separate the threads and place each one between two toothpicks. Pull each thread across the box between the toothpicks on the other side.

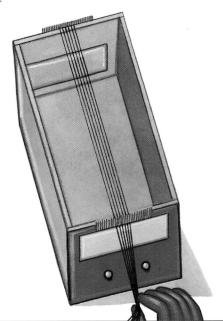

**4** When all the threads are straight across the loom, pull them tight. Fasten them around the paper fasteners in a figure eight pattern. Stretch a rubber band around them to keep them from coming loose.

**5** Position the loom the long way in front of you. Thread your needle with 1 m (3 ft.) of thread. Tie the thread to the top left loom thread leaving a 10-cm (4-in.) tail.

**6** Pass the needle under the loom threads to the right side.

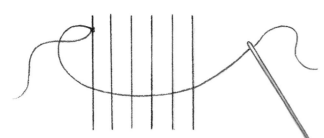

**7** Following your pattern (see page 34), thread on beads and let them slide down the beading thread. Guide them with your fingers so that one bead goes between two loom threads.

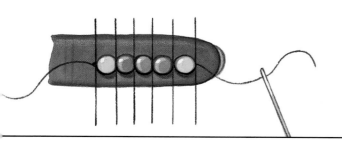

**8** Pass the needle through the beads from right to left. Make sure your needle passes *through* each bead and *above* each loom thread. Keep the thread taut and smooth.

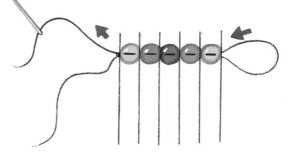

**9** Pass the needle and thread under the loom threads back to the right side. Thread on more beads and keep going. Try to use only smooth, evenly sized beads. When you need to change thread, weave the end back through a couple of rows of beads. Trim the thread.

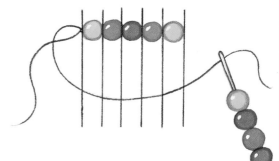

**10** Cut a new piece of thread, knot it on the left side and continue beading. Weave in the tail when you have beaded a few more rows. Turn to page 40 to find out how to finish off your loomwork.

# Loopy-loom bracelet

*This jazzed-up loom bracelet is fun to make. Add any charms, pendants or interesting beads you have collected.*

1 Using E beads, make a plain bracelet four or five beads wide. Leave it on the loom.

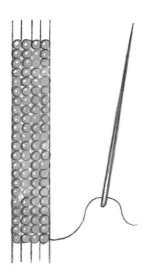

2 If you still have a beading thread on the go, use it. If it is getting short, weave it in, and start a new thread. Tie the new thread at one of the four corners of your bracelet.

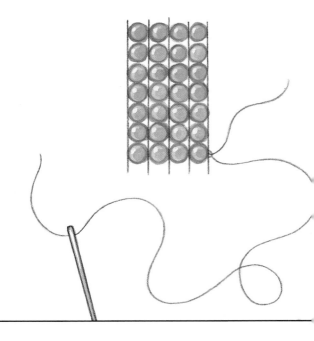

3 Thread your needle through the closest E bead. Thread on five seed beads, an E bead or other larger bead, and five more seed beads.

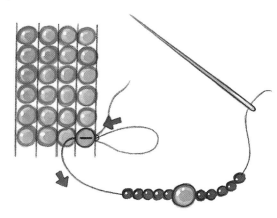

4 Bring the needle back through the same corner bead in the same direction, to form a loop. Pull it tight.

5 Poke the needle into another bead in the same row, perhaps choosing to make a loop on every other bead in every other row. Always make sure your beading thread does not show by drawing it through other beads to get where you're going. Make another loop by threading on the same pattern of beads and re-entering the loom bead. Continue making loops on the bracelet.

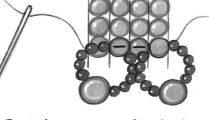

6 When you are finished, weave in all the ends. Trim and secure the ends with nail polish.

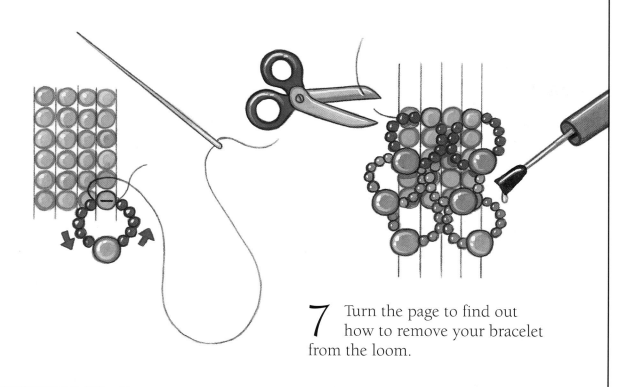

7 Turn the page to find out how to remove your bracelet from the loom.

# Finishing

*There are many ways to finish a piece of loomwork. Begin by securing the knots and beads at both ends with nail polish. Then unwind and trim the loom threads.*

● For a bracelet, you can gather up the loom threads and tie them in an overhand knot as close to the beadwork as possible. Do this on both ends. You can then tie on a clasp or simply tie the ends together around your wrist. Add nail polish to secure the knots.

● You can also tightly braid the loom threads and tie the bracelet around your wrist.

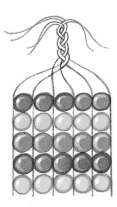

● Another way to finish off a bracelet is to thread a few seed beads onto each thread or pair of threads. Tie on a clasp and weave the ends back through the beads, or tie the ends together around your wrist. Trim the threads and secure the knots with nail polish.

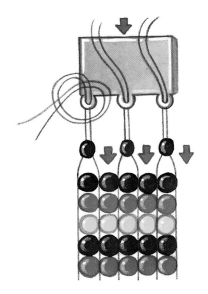